PRAYER AND THE WORD OF GOD

Breakthrough Prayer Studies for Small Groups

CYNTHIA HYLE BEZEK

PRAYERSHOP PUBLISHING

Terre Haute, Indiana

PrayerShop Publishing is the publishing arm of Harvest Prayer Ministries and the Church Prayer Leaders Network. Harvest Prayer Ministries exists to transform lives through teaching prayer. Its online prayer store, www.prayershop.org, has more than 500 prayer resources available for purchase.

ISBN: 978-1-935012-54-2

Some of the anecdotal illustrations in this book are true to life and are included with the permissions of the persons involved. All other illustrations are composites of real situations and any resemblance to people living or dead is coincidental.

All Scripture quotations, unless otherwise indicated, are taken from the Holy Bible, New International Version®, NIV®. Copyright ©1973, 1978, 1984 by Biblica, Inc. Used by permission of Zondervan. All rights reserved worldwide. www.zondervan.com

Scripture quotations marked "NLT" are taken from the *Holy Bible*, New Living Translation, copyright © 1996, 2004, 2007 by Tyndale House Foundation. Used by permission of Tyndale House Publishers, Inc., Carol Stream, Illinois 60188. All rights reserved.

Scripture quotations marked "MSG" are from *THE MESSAGE*. Copyright © 1993, 1994, 1995, 1996, 2000, 2001, 2002 by Eugene H. Peterson. Used by permission of NavPress Publishing Group.

Scripture quotations marked "NRSV" are from the *New Revised Standard Version Bible*, © 1989, Division of Christian Education of the National Council of the Churches of Christ in the United States of America. Used by permission. All rights reserved.

KJV – public domain

Printed in the United States of America

1 2 3 4 5 | 2018 2017 2016 2015 2014

Table of Contents

Introduction

PRAYER AND THE BIBLE go hand in hand. But not in the way I used to think. Perhaps like you, I was taught that "we speak to God through prayer and He speaks to us through His Word." I still believe that's true—as far as it goes. But I've also come to realize that teaching is incomplete and can even be misleading.

Most important, the Bible is God's revelation of Himself. In Scripture, we learn what kind of God He is: What He values. What He thinks. What He feels—including what He feels about *us*. We discover what He has done. What He still wants to do. How He invites us to participate with Him. How He responds to us. We learn what kind of *Person* He is. Our conversations with Him flow out of that knowledge. We learn that the purpose of His Word is to bring us life through relationship with Him.

Also in the Bible we get to see how other people—men and women like us—talked with God. What they said to Him, how they related with Him, and, in turn, how He related back with them. We learn from these examples of other people who knew God what relating with Him can be like.

Some of their prayers are recorded in Scripture, providing us with rich and varied examples of what prayer can be like. Sometimes, as in the Psalms, for example, we find words to borrow, words that express our hearts even better than we can.

Typical teaching about the role of Scripture in prayer includes a study of biblical prayers—especially the Lord's Prayer—or perhaps discussion about how to pray the will and promises of God as revealed in the Bible. This study also explores those important topics. But first we'll go into more foundational lessons that encourage us to think about how the Bible can open up our conversations with God. How do we view the Bible? Is it a rule book, a love letter, a narrative of the cosmos? Is it true and authoritative, or is it subjective? The way we view Scripture will shape the way we pray.

This study will also explore how we can engage with God about what He has said and receive it in ways that truly transform us. How we can invite the Holy Spirit to initiate with us according to God's written Word and interpret it to the specific situations of our lives. And we can learn to stand against the enemy's schemes to twist God's Word and use it against us.

FOUNDATIONS

Before we begin that exploration, I want you to know some foundations this study is built on.

First, the study assumes that prayer—at its most basic level—is a relationship with God. And God Himself is very relational. That's why, in the pages ahead, we'll talk so much about relationship and about communicating with God as a real Person.

Also, prayer is a two-way interaction. When you pray, you're talking with a present God who has committed Himself to live with you 24/7. You'll be encouraged, in your prayer conversations, to talk with God and then be quiet and listen to what He says to you in reply.

Finally, because prayer is two-way relational conversation, prayer can happen in a variety of formats. We'll talk about many different modes of praying so you can enjoy new ways of talking with God. Although some of these modes may be new, I encourage you to involve yourself—your whole self—in the ways the lessons invite you to. If you're asked to pray, please take time to pray. If you're asked how you feel about something, please search your heart and try to discover that. If you're asked to be honest about your experiences with God, please be honest, even if you have been disappointed or confused.

STUDY OVERVIEW

To help us accomplish these goals, each lesson includes four regular components:

- **Think about It** is an opening question that invites you to reflect on how you have interacted with the theme of the lesson in your life so far.
- **Invite God to Speak** gives you a Scripture and a different way of using it as the basis for a conversation with God each week.
- **Going Deeper** is the Bible study portion of each lesson.
- **Your Turn** offers several prayer exercises that you can try to begin experiencing the themes more deeply in your own conversations with God.

All four components are very important if you want to really *get* the concepts explored in this study. If you want to hear from God through Scripture, then another obvious necessity would be for you actually to be taking in regular portions of Scripture. Perhaps you already have a method for doing this. If you do not, consider the suggestions in Appendix A, "Bible Reading Plan."

More than anything, Scripture has formed the way I pray. Through it, God has invited me into deeper, more relational, increasingly creative, and enjoyable ways of talking with and experiencing Him. It's my prayer that through this study He will do the same for you.

How to Get the Most from This Study

THIS STUDY IS DESIGNED to provide practical, hands-on opportunities for you to grow deeper in your relationship with God through prayer. With that in mind, realize that you will get the most out of the study if you do each lesson on your own and come to your group time prepared to share what you have experienced and where you may be struggling. (Of course you may also use this study on your own. Even though use in a group is recommended, individual study will also provide much benefit.)

During the week you'll explore how God has revealed Himself through Scripture and you'll interact with Him through prayer. As a guideline, plan to spend about twenty to thirty minutes a day in the lesson. You will be asked to read Scripture, reflect, respond, and try out what you learn in prayer practice. The format of your assignments could make an ideal devotional time, if you'd like to think of it that way. Spending time on your lesson every day saves you last-minute frustration, and, more important, reinforces a pattern of relating personally to God daily.

How you divide up a lesson over a week is up to you. You can do a section a day, or you can do several sections at once. The prayer practices, however, should not be attempted in one sitting, so pace yourself so that you allow several days for prayer. Since the object of this study is not to learn *about* prayer but actually to pray, the prayer exercises are *essential*. If you only work through the questions and participate in group discussion, you will miss the whole point of the study. So when the lesson prompts you to talk with God about something, *please talk with God.* You learn to pray *by praying.*

As you answer questions, discuss, and pray, you may notice this study is different from others you have done and it might require a different approach from what you are accustomed to. Many studies are aimed at gaining information about the Bible or a spiritual topic. This one aims at transforming how you relate with God. So, as you work your way through this study guide, I'd encourage you to enter into an experiential, discovery mode. Instead of just "trying to get homework done" or "reading passages to write down a right answer," I'm inviting you—challenging you, even—to let these lessons guide you into real, relational conversations with God. At first, it may be hard to bypass your usual "Bible study mode." I understand! I've approached many Bible studies as quests to find answers and master information. If you tend to approach studies with that mind-set, be conscious of switching into a different, relational, framework when you open this book.

Relational transformation will happen if you are willing to adopt several important approaches:

- Be honest with yourself and God about where you are in your relationship with Him and how you feel about talking with Him. Prayer is a vulnerable topic for many people—even pastors and spiritual leaders. Many of us (maybe even *most* of us) are not where we want to be when it comes to prayer. If you are willing to be honest about your disappointments, frustrations, and struggles, this study can move you closer to where you hope to be.
- Be willing to be stretched. Some of the questions and exercises will move you out of your comfort zone. Please enter in, even if you are doubtful or unsure. As people have done this study, they reported that *if they were willing to try the prayer responses, they*

were surprised at how God met them and how talking with God became more rewarding.

• Respect where you are—and where others in your group are—on your journey with God in prayer. Don't be afraid to share your weaknesses with other members. At the same time, be sensitive when other members share their weaknesses. Don't try to coach them with what works for *you*. Let the Holy Spirit do the coaching. Help create a safe environment for everyone to be vulnerable.

What I will share with you in this study only begins to scratch the surface of how you can relate with God. But that's okay. My goal is to ignite in you a passion to know and relate to God—a passion that makes you look forward to having all of eternity to get to know our amazing, infinite God!

Note to Leaders: Visit www.harvestprayer.com/resources/free-downloads to download a Leader's Guide. You'll find detailed information in the guide for how to begin and facilitate this study.

IMPORTANT TERMS

We have several different words and phrases that we use to talk about the Bible. We tend to use them interchangeably, although there are some distinctions that are important to consider. Following are some of the terms for the Bible that you will encounter in this study.

Bible. This familiar term (which never occurs in the book we call the Bible) comes from the Greek word *biblion* ("book" or "roll"). *Biblion* in turn derives from *Byblos,* which refers to the papyrus plant from which writing material was made in ancient times. Eventually the plural term *biblia* was used to refer to all the books of the Old and New Testaments.

Scripture (or Scriptures). *Scripture* also comes from a Greek term—*grafh*—meaning "A writing, that which is written." When we use it today, in the plural, it refers to the collection of sacred writings as a whole—the Old and New Testaments. However, often in the New Testament when it is used, it refers to just the Old Testament.

The Law. Although the term can suggest a certain part of the Scriptures, it's important to note that Jesus (and possibly some of the New Testament writers) also used it to refer to the entire Old Testament (e.g., John 10:34; 12:34).

God's Word, the Word of God. We often use these terms to refer to the Bible, and it's totally appropriate to do so. However, there's an important caution to take into consideration. "God's Word" can also mean other things. God brought the world into existence by speaking His Word (2 Peter 3:7). The LORD spoke His Word through the prophets (Hebrews 1:1). Jesus is the Word of God (John 1:1, 14). God gives His words to us through His Spirit (Matthew 10:20; 1 Corinthians 2:10-13). For the purposes of this study, when we wish for "God's Word" or "Word of God" to refer to the Bible, we will say "God's written Word" or "the written Word of God." When we are talking of God speaking to an individual, including Him speaking to you, we will use God's word, lowercase.

God's Word Brings Life

I LOVE THE BIBLE. Although God speaks to me in many different ways, God's written Word remains the primary way I hear from Him and forms the basis of all I know and enjoy about Him. Receiving God's Word brings me into life-giving relationship with Him, and that relationship is the basis of prayer itself. But just reading Scripture does not automatically bring about a deep and delightful prayer life—at least that wasn't the case for me. I had to learn how to read it, how to engage with God about it, and how to receive from Him through it. In this lesson I will share with you some of the things I learned that helped me to grow closer to God through His Word and prayer.

THINK ABOUT IT

Consider your experience with the Bible. These are some questions you could reflect on: Why do you suppose that God's Word deeply penetrates some people while others seem to let it go in one ear and out the other? What has been your experience with reading and hearing God's Word? How does (or doesn't) it affect the way you pray?

INVITE GOD TO SPEAK

Scripture provides rich fodder for prayer. Even verses and passages that are not prayers in themselves can provide inspiration for your own prayers. Read the following verses. First ask the Holy Spirit to highlight one for you. Then notice what seems to jump off the page at you or stir a thought or feeling.

- [The disciples who had been walking along the road to Emmaus] asked each other, "Were not our hearts burning within us while [Jesus] talked with us on the road and opened the Scriptures to us?" (Luke 24:32)
- And we also thank God continually because, when you received the word of God, which you heard from us, you accepted it not as a human word, but as it actually is, the word of God, which is indeed at work in you who believe. (1 Thessalonians 2:13)
- And humbly accept the word planted in you, which can save you. (James 1:21)

1. Which one stands out to you?

2. What hope or desire does it stir in you?

3. Write a personalized prayer based on the Scripture you chose. If God has stirred specific hopes or desires in you, include these in your prayer. Make sure that your prayer asks God to create in you some kind of heart response. Remember, the goal is not just information but life change.

After you've written your prayer, pray it often throughout this week. If you've not prayed Scripture like this before, here is an example of what it might sound like: *Jesus, I don't know if my heart has ever "burned within me" as I've read or heard Scripture. But I want my relationship with You to be more than just intellectual. I want my heart to be affected by knowing You. So would You please open Scripture to me in a way that causes my heart to respond?*

GOING DEEPER

Ever since I was a teenager, I have made daily Bible reading a high priority. But the way I read has changed a lot over the years. Early on I read the Bible essentially the same way I'd read any other book. I'd read a chapter or two a day—sometimes more—put a bookmark where I left off, and forget about it until I picked it back up the next day.

Somewhere in my twenties, I decided to implement a plan to help me retain more. I began disciplining myself to pause at the end of each day's reading and ask some questions: What does this passage say? What commands or promises does it offer? How can I apply this to my life? I'd journal my responses, pray about them, and try my best to live them. This was an improvement over the superficial reading I'd done before.

However, I still did not grow much in my relationship with God or my prayer life. In fact, sometimes my intake of the Bible may have actually hindered it. Let me explain.

For many of those years, the Bible was little more than a rule book for me. It explained the way to eternal life and then laid out a pattern for living a good and righteous life. I tried very hard to obey the many commandments it contained, but always found myself missing the mark—especially when it came to commands that required me to forgive seventy times seven times, return good for evil, give to everyone who asks, speak only words that edify, be thankful for everything, think only thoughts that are noble and lovely, pray without ceasing, and on and on. I'd faithfully read my Bible every day, only to watch the lists of what I needed to improve get longer and longer.

Don't misunderstand, I knew I was saved by God's grace alone and not by any good works I might manage to pull off. But sadly, those theological understandings had little effect. Because the Bible seemed to be forever pointing out my shortcomings, I constantly felt as if God were disappointed with me. Can you imagine what my praying was like in those days? I sometimes avoided God. When I did pray, I felt guilt, shame, and anxiety. My prayers consisted mostly of confession and pleading to help me do better.

Obviously, not everyone reads the Bible with that perspective. I recently talked with a woman who also has read the Bible every day for a long time. She told me she views the Bible as God's love letter to her. Her approach to the Bible is to read until she finds an encouraging part and not worry about the rest of it. While her practice brings more hope than mine did, I question whether it's broad enough.

Other folks I've known read the Bible almost as an academic exercise. Their reading is intellectually stimulating, gives them interesting information about life in biblical times, and fuels their thinking about theological viewpoints and end-time theories. But it doesn't necessarily deepen their relationships with God.

And, happily, there are a few people I've met who have had altogether positive experiences with Bible reading. They are equally receptive to encouragement and correction, and they apply what they learn about God to their lives in ways that deepens their relationship with Him and improves their relationships with others. Even these blessed individuals, however, will usually admit that coming to enjoy Scripture like this has been a process and journey.

1. Read Matthew 4:4; John 20:30-31; and Galatians 3:23-25. Based on these verses, why do you think God gave us the Scriptures?

2. Read John 5:39-40. Jesus addressed these comments to Jews who would have known the Scriptures well. But they missed the point. In all their study of the Scriptures, what did they miss?

3. These leaders missed out on the life that comes to us through Jesus. How do you think this could have happened?

4. Jesus said that Scripture pointed to Him, and that when we come to Him we have life. Many of us have become used to thinking about prayer merely in terms of praising God, confessing sin, or presenting prayer requests to Him. What role does our relationship with Jesus have in our prayers?

5. If a person misses the point about Scripture, how might that affect his or her prayer life?

You're probably starting to see the point I'm trying to make, but let me state it anyway: reading, studying, memorizing, exegeting, even obeying the Scriptures does not automatically guarantee relationship with God. Why not? Because some of us misunderstand their primary purpose. God gave us the Bible so we could know Him. He wanted to reveal Himself to us and invite us into relationship with Himself and His Son, Jesus, through the Holy Spirit. If we miss this crucial point, as I did for a long time, we miss just about everything.

There is another crucial point that I was missing. In the days when I viewed the Bible primarily as an instruction book for being a good Christian, I viewed prayer mainly as a discipline of praise and intercession that God expected from serious Christians. I may not have been able to admit that to you at the time, but deep down, that's how it was for me. I didn't see either the Bible or prayer as the source of life and satisfying relationship. Now I know that prayer—at its most basic level—is a relationship with God. Prayer is a two-way interaction. When you pray, you're entering a conversation where you talk with God and He responds to you and talks with you.

This is why our approach to the Bible is so foundational to our prayer life. The Bible is one of the key ways we hear God speaking to us.

HEARING GOD THROUGH THE BIBLE

Before I came to this realization, if you'd asked me if God spoke to me through the Bible, I'd have said yes, of course He does. But if you probed a little about what kinds of things I actually heard Him say through His Word, I would have had to confess that I heard a whole lot of conviction, correction, and admonishment to do better. I wouldn't have been able to tell you much about hearing His fatherly affirmation, affection, support, or encouragement. Not because He wasn't saying it, and not because it wasn't in the Scriptures, but simply because I had the wrong approach.

1. Reflect on your experience of hearing God through the Bible. Do you hear mostly rules and commands like I did? Do you listen primarily to the pleasant parts and skip over the rest? Do you read it like a textbook? Other?

2. What kinds of things does God usually say to you through the Bible?

3. How does what you hear Him say affect the way you feel, respond to Him in prayer, or live your life?

I'm glad to let you know that my way of reading Scripture has changed considerably over the years. One of the happy results has been encouraging changes in the way I talk to God. The Bible has become a source of life and hope for me—and remains the primary way I get to know, hear from, and commune with God, which has revolutionized my prayer life. The Bible is part of God's prayer conversation with me. Now I hear in a much more complete and life-giving way. One huge thing that has helped me is learning to receive God's word—letting His words of life saturate me and become part of me.

RECEIVING WHAT GOD SAYS TO YOU

1. Read the familiar stories of how two different people, Zechariah (Luke 1:5-20) and Mary (Luke 1:26-38), responded when they heard the word of the Lord.

    a. What did Zechariah say?

    b. How did Mary respond?

    c. How were their responses similar?

d. How were their responses different?

2. If you were to hear an incredible but wonderful message from God, how would you respond? Do you think you would be more like Zechariah or Mary? Why?

3. What do you suppose accounts for the differences in the ways Zechariah and Mary received God's word to them? (The passages do not actually give us this information—you'll need to speculate.)

Zechariah kept what Gabriel said at arm's length. Mary accepted and received it. When I use the word *receive*, I am suggesting a heart, mind, soul, and strength taking in of the Word of God in a way that it becomes part of you and brings about lasting inner transformation. This kind of receiving will result in a whole-person change in your thoughts, feelings, decisions, and actions. It will change your prayers, because you will not be able to dismiss what He is saying as irrelevant to you. His words will challenge, comfort, convict, or stretch you on a deep, heart level, and you will want to, even need to, respond to Him from your heart.

Many people hear and read God's written Word. They may be able to give intelligent, helpful, and accurate explanations of it. They may be able to quote it and even write books or give sermons on it. But that does not mean they have *received* it. John talks about this phenomenon in John 1. He says that the Word became flesh and dwelt among us. Some people received the Word and became children of God. Others, however, did not receive the Word—ironically these non-receivers were the most religious people of Jesus' day, the Jews, who studied and knew the Scriptures cover to cover. But they did not receive. Their hearts were not changed by what they heard, and they did not receive life and blessing as a result.

Taking in and receiving what God says to us through His word will not result in a glib response. Sometimes we will not like what we hear, or, like Zechariah and Mary, we will have questions about it. This is a normal part of taking in God's words to us.

4. Both Zechariah and Mary asked questions upon hearing the word of God to them. But God's response to them was different. What do you think might account for this difference?

5. Though God probably isn't sending angels with messages to you or me, we are talking with God when we pray and hearing Him talk with us. What might make you hesitate to ask God questions about the things you sense He is saying to you through His written Word?

6. Why might God actually enjoy your questions?

Like Zechariah, I have found it hard to receive from both people and

God. When a friend or colleague would say, "You did a great job!" or "Have you thought about doing _____? You'd be really good at it!" I was likely to blush and change the subject or perhaps smile and give a polite "Thanks," but to myself say "Whatever!" and brush them off. Regrettably, I would often do the same thing when God spoke to me. He might say, "You are my treasured possession" (Deuteronomy 7:6), or "I am calling you to do great things for me" (John 14:12), but it was not uncommon for me to ignore Him or change the subject. Sometimes I even argued with Him: "Who, me? Have You forgotten how I always seem to mess things up?" It comforts me a little to know that I was in good company—Moses and Gideon (to give just two biblical examples) did pretty much the same thing (see Exodus 3:7-4:17 and Judges 6:11-40).

Still, Moses and Gideon did eventually receive the messages God had for them—and I am learning, too. I believe a key to receiving is to engage in honest dialogue with God. Like Moses, Gideon—and even Mary—I am slowly learning not to brush off and ignore what God says to me, but rather to talk with Him about it. I tell Him how what He says makes me feel. I share my concerns and reservations with Him. I ask Him questions about things I don't understand. I tell Him I want to receive what He is saying, but it's hard. I ask Him to help me receive and to reveal what hinders me. These are some of my most valued prayer times with God.

When I talk to Him in this way, He has always been faithful to help me. I've never sensed Him getting upset or impatient with me because I couldn't instantly accept His words to me. I think that's because He knows I have an open heart that wants to receive from Him. Sometimes our conversation goes on for days, weeks, months, or even longer (some things are harder to receive than others!).

7. Luke 2:19 and 2:51 tells us about a habit Mary engaged in that may

give us a hint about how she was able to receive God's word. What is this habit?

8. What do you think pondering or treasuring in one's heart means? How might a person practice this habit?

9. How might pondering (versus merely reading or hearing one time) help a person receive God's words more deeply? (For more about pondering, go to Appendix B: "Suggestions for Meditating on God's Word.")

As I ponder God's word to me, I keep a conversation going with Him about it. I read the Bible, the Holy Spirit highlights a portion for me, and I have questions. I ask God a question and then I listen for His reply. I watch for His answer, and I ask Him more questions. This extended conversation with Him is praying, even though it looks different from when I'm praying for the needs of my son or a friend.

When I do this, I am usually able to receive from Him—and without exception, I've always been glad I did. The more I am able to deeply receive His word to me, the more I find myself trusting Him. And that means that I feel more confident and secure, I am more able to step out with Him into the things He has for me to do and be, and I find more peace, satisfaction, and joy in my life with Him. Loving God is becoming more heart-soul-mind-and-strength for me in direct proportion to my ability to receive His word to me. I'm learning that receiving is a good thing! I'm learning that engaging with God through His word in this manner is a deeply relational and satisfying way to pray.

YOUR TURN

The "Your Turn" section in each lesson gives you an opportunity to interact with God in conversation—in other words, to pray *relationally*—about what you are learning. Working with these exercises is very important if you want God to actually change you through this study.

Please choose one of the following exercises to talk with God about this week. If you have time, do both.

PRAYER EXERCISE 1: Practice Receiving What God Has to Say to You

Is there a verse or biblical truth that God is currently using with you or emphasizing for you? Write it below, and we'll use it to practice receiving.

If you have trouble thinking of a Scripture to receive, consider these possibilities:

- As far as the east is from the west, so far has he removed our transgressions from us. (Psalm 103:12)
- "Therefore I tell you, do not worry about your life, what you

will eat or drink; or about your body, what you will wear. Is not life more important than food, and the body more important than clothes? Look at the birds of the air; they do not sow or reap or store away in barns, and yet your heavenly Father feeds them. Are you not much more valuable than they? Who of you by worrying can add a single hour to his life?

"And why do you worry about clothes? See how the lilies of the field grow. They do not labor or spin. Yet I tell you that not even Solomon in all his splendor was dressed like one of these. If that is how God clothes the grass of the field, which is here today and tomorrow is thrown into the fire, will he not much more clothe you, O you of little faith?" (Matthew 6:25-30).

• "Come to me, all you who are weary and burdened, and I will give you rest. Take my yoke upon you and learn from me, for I am gentle and humble in heart, and you will find rest for your souls. For my yoke is easy and my burden is light" (Matthew 11:28-30).

• "I no longer call you servants, because a servant does not know his master's business. Instead, I have called you friends, for everything that I learned from my Father I have made known to you" (John 15:15).

• And we know that in all things God works for the good of those who love him, who have been called according to his purpose (Romans 8:28).

• And my God will meet all your needs according to his glorious riches in Christ Jesus (Philippians 4:19).

1. Read the passage several times, slowly, with pauses between ideas. Is there anything that jumps out to you? Write it below.

2. Notice emotions and questions that arise from the part that jumped out to you. What do you feel? What questions do you have?

3. Tell God how you feel or ask Him one of your questions. Then sit silently for a few minutes. Listen for His response. Do you sense Him saying or doing anything in reply to what you shared? Write it down. Do you feel like your heart engaged with God? Are you able to receive? If you are finding it difficult to receive, move on to "Difficulty with Receiving," below.

DIFFICULTY WITH RECEIVING

Receiving what God says to us isn't always simple as we would like it to be. Sometimes we can be blocked in ways we don't realize.

- Look at the sidebar, "Hindrances to Receiving" on pages 28-29. Ask God to show you if any of these hindrances are blocking you from more fully receiving His word to you.
- Ask Him for help in getting through these obstacles, then ask Him what your part is.
- Listen for His response. Keep the dialogue going and act on whatever steps you are able to. Make notes here of what you sense Him saying to you.

HINDRANCES TO RECEIVING

It seems that some people are blessed with innocent, childlike faith that easily believes and receives from God. Many of us, however, find believing and receiving more difficult. There are many reasons for our struggle. Here are some common ones:

Rationalistic thinking. Our education and culture train us to accept only what is "logical" and can be scientifically proven. Even though we *say* we believe in a supernatural God who intervenes in our world, many of us find it hard to believe anything that cannot be concretely proven—including things like love, forgiveness, and favor.

Didn't know. For some of us, it simply has never occurred to us that God's written Word is something personal that He means for us to receive. We've never had anyone tell us that before. We've never seen it modeled. We just never thought about it.

Independence. If we pride ourselves in being self-sufficient, then we will not sense much need for the things God wants to say to us and give to us. We may hear His words, but because we think we're doing just fine and don't really need any input, we let them go unheeded and unreceived.

Woundedness. Sometimes God says things to us that seem "too good to be true." They are outside our experience of how the world works and how we expect to be treated. If, for example, we've experienced much rejection in our lives, it may be hard for us to receive God's unconditional acceptance.

Religious perspective. Some of us are so busy trying to figure out what God expects of us, what "rules" we need to follow, and how to "be a good Christian" that we miss the relationship God desires to have with us. God's word to us is always more about relationship than rules. If we don't have that relational perspective, we'll probably find it difficult to receive much from Him.

Enemy deception. Satan's earliest trick in the book is to get us to doubt God's word. "Did God *really* say . . ." he asked Eve, planting in her a seed of fatal doubt (Genesis 3:1). If we are not aware of his evil schemes, we will let the enemy talk us out of receiving God's truth and goodness for us.

Previous disappointment. Proverbs 13:12 says that "hope deferred makes the heart sick." This may be what happened to Zechariah. He'd prayed for a child for decades and God seemed not to be hearing. When God finally *did* respond to him, Zechariah's heart had stopped hoping. He could not receive God's word because of years of disappointment.

PRAYER EXERCISE 2: Treasure God's Word

Develop the skill—and joy—of meditating on God's Word, as Mary did. Choose a Bible verse or passage to ponder. It could be a favorite psalm, a verse your pastor recently spoke on, or something you read in your quiet time. Once you have selected a passage, turn to Appendix B and choose a few of the ideas given there to help you ponder God's word to you. Journal about your experience, or share it with a friend. For more tips on how to listen to God, refer to Appendix C.

The Holy Spirit,
Our Come-Alongside Interpreter and Initiator

Note: You will be invited to practice the principles you learn in this lesson for several days prior to your group's next meeting. It's good to know this now so you can plan your time accordingly.

TWO WEEKS AFTER MY SON graduated from college, he moved home for a season, repopulating my empty nest. I'd lived alone for three years, so his moving required a considerable adjustment. A happy one! I love my son; we work and play together well, and we genuinely enjoy one another's company. Still, his near-constant presence often caught me off guard. I had almost gotten used to doing life alone when, suddenly, there was someone else who had input, ideas, and desires I needed to consider. I had to learn not to jump when, absorbed in deep thought, a loud "Hey, Mom!" interrupted and startled me. But there was also the happy realization that when I couldn't get my MP3 player or camera to upload, when there was a foot of snow on the driveway, or when I was going on a business trip and needed a cat sitter, I didn't have to figure out the solution by myself. My son would be glad to help.

My son initiated things ("Want to watch a movie?" "Are we going to have someone over for dinner again soon?"). He interpreted things, helping me to read and understand owner's manuals, financial statements, and websites. He reminded me of things, like where I put my cell phone or that I'd promised to do something for someone. He needed things—the car, help with his résumé, a sounding board to talk through prospects for his future.

In short, I had to adapt my life to accommodate another person— but the adjustment was good for me. Sharing life with my son was a blessing. I'd almost forgotten how much richer life could be when shared with another.

This experience of adjusting my life in order to share it with another person helped me to understand what it is like to do life with God and maintain an ongoing conversation with the Holy Spirit.

THINK ABOUT IT

Do you tend to do life solo (making your own decisions, handling and figuring out things by yourself) or in partnership with another person or other people? (Keep in mind that doing life solo doesn't depend on your marital or roommate status. Some married folks are Lone Rangers while some singles regularly partner with others.) What are the advantages and disadvantages of your preferred mode?

INVITE GOD TO SPEAK

When we receive Jesus as our Savior, the Holy Spirit takes up residence inside us, always with us, promising never, ever to leave us. Many of us love knowing that He is our ever-present, Divine Companion. But He is more than that.

He is also our Divine Interpreter, teaching us and helping us to understand the things God is saying to us.

And in another very real sense, He is our Divine Interrupter. A nicer way of saying it might be "Divine Initiator." He has this way of popping up when we don't expect Him, reminding us, pointing things out to us, prompting, convicting, guiding, and even seeming to nag at times.

Jesus talks about these roles of the Holy Spirit in John 14: "But the Counselor, the Holy Spirit, whom the Father will send in my name, will teach you [interpret] all things and will remind you [interrupt, initiate a conversation about] of everything I have said to you" (verse 26, comments in brackets mine.)

Take some time to meditate on John 14:15-26. Here is one way you could do it:

- Read the passage slowly, out loud, to familiarize yourself with it. After you finish, sit silently for two or three minutes, pondering what you read. Don't try to "figure it out." Don't try to pray about it. Just let it roll gently around your heart and mind.
- Now read the passage again, in the same slow, out-loud fashion. When you finish, sit silently for another two or three minutes. Ask yourself, "What does Jesus seem like in this passage?" "What is He inviting me to?" "What sticks out to me in this passage?" Continue to meditate on the word, phrase, or idea that stuck out to you.
- For your third reading (done in the same manner) consider what the Holy Spirit might be stirring in your heart. What feelings are you experiencing? Are there hopes or longings that rise? Talk to God about whatever you find happening in your heart.
- Do a final reading in the same manner. After the reading, invite God to work in you today and this week to bring about whatever it is that He wants for you in connection with these verses. Open your hands to Him as you pray, as a gesture of your desire

to receive from Him the things that only He can give to you and do for you.

1. Summarize your experiences of praying this passage this way. This might not seem like prayer as you're used to it, but what you've just done actually is prayer. Prayer is simply talking to God. Here, you've used the Bible passage to talk to God and let Him talk to you. What was it like for you?

Note: This reading method is called *Lectio Divina*. See Appendix D for more information and ideas on how to engage with God through Scripture using this centuries-old method.

GOING DEEPER

In the previous lesson, we saw that God's Word is meant to bring us life and bring us into relationship with Him. The relationship that comes from this encounter in His life-giving Word becomes the basis for our prayers. In order for that to happen, we need God to bring His Word to life for us. Through His Holy Spirit, that's exactly what He does.

The Greek word translated as "Counselor" in the New International Version's rendering of John 14:26 is *paraclete*. In other versions, it's translated in different ways: Helper, Counselor, Comforter, Advocate, and Friend are some of the common ones. The word means literally "to come alongside." God's Spirit helps us communicate with God by coming alongside to interpret God's word to us and initiate conversations with us from it.

1. What are some of the ways the Holy Spirit can help us hear, understand, and benefit from God's Word? Look up the following passages and jot down what you notice.

a. John 14:26

b. John 15:26

c. Romans 8:26

d. 1 Corinthians 2:12

e. 1 Thessalonians 1:5

The following account illustrates some ways the Holy Spirit encouraged, taught, and led me through Scripture.

> *I was the guest of honor at a dinner recently where most of the other guests didn't know each other well, if at all. At first I was concerned about how the evening would go: Would people find things to talk about? Would the shy ones feel comfortable? As the evening progressed, I was amazed at what happened. People connected. They asked questions, shared stories, suggested ideas, offered encouragement.* Wow! *I thought.* Sit people down at a table with good food in a relaxed atmosphere and look what God does! Here is community in the making!

The next morning I pondered this with God, thinking and journaling about the power of hospitality in developing and deepening relationships. Then, since I usually read my Bible systematically, I opened my Bible to where I had left off the day before—3 John. This is what I read: "Dear friend, when you extend hospitality to Christian brothers and sisters, even when they are strangers, you make the faith visible. They've made a full report back to the church here, a message about your love. It's good work you're doing, helping these travelers on their way, hospitality worthy of God himself!" (5-6, MSG)

"Okay, Holy Spirit, You have my attention," I said to God. "You obviously want to talk to me about hospitality. What should I be seeing, feeling, or understanding? Speak, Lord, I'm listening."

I don't always read the study notes in my Bible, but this time I did. I was once again amazed. The commentator listed the many times Jesus ministered to people around a meal. He mentioned many parables Jesus told while seated at the dinner table. He wrote about the hospitality of Abraham and pointed out Scriptures that advocate practicing hospitality. He went so far as to say, "Daily meals with family, friends, and guests, acts of hospitality, every one, are the most natural and frequent settings for working out the personal and social implications of salvation" (Eugene H. Peterson in Conversations: The Message with Its Translator, p. 1944).

"Yes, Lord?" I asked, after reading all this. And I sensed Him encourage me about the gift of hospitality He'd given me years earlier. That gift had nearly gone dormant during the years of my husband's illness and my subsequent widowhood. Now, as a single, working woman, hospitality felt like a whole lot of work for not much reward. But God was clearly asking me to explore it again. As I prayed about this, new ideas and ways to "repurpose" the *way I offered hospitality came to mind. I felt anticipation start to build.*

The next day in Sunday school, our class spent time in the account in Luke 10 of Jesus sending out the seventy-two. Different parts of the passage jumped out to different people, but verses 8-9 caught my attention: "When you enter a town and are received, eat what they set before you, heal anyone who is sick, and tell them, 'God's kingdom is right on your doorstep!'" Wow, here we are again, three days in a row, I mused. Eat and heal. There is something powerful about taking meals together. Hospitality and healing go together! I never saw that before. Now I was getting excited.

I continued discussing these things with God for quite a while, and even now He is still speaking to me. Clearly He is rebirthing something important in my life.

2. Notice how the Holy Spirit interrupted/initiated with me and also how He interpreted/taught God's written Word to me. Underline the different ways the Holy Spirit spoke to me in the story you just read. (I notice at least four.)

3. How many of these ways were connected with Scripture?

4. How many of these ways were connected with prayer?

5. Think of how the Holy Spirit uses the Scriptures with you. Give examples of how the Holy Spirit has

    a. interrupted you, initiated with you, or reminded you

    b. interpreted the Bible to you or taught you

There are different ways the Holy Spirit comes alongside us as we interact with Scripture. Here are some:

- He may invite us into dialogue (prayer in a two-way conversation) as we read God's Word; we might ask Him questions about it or He might bring applications to our mind.
- He might bring up a topic we haven't been thinking about in order to guide us into a certain path.
- He might bring to mind a Scripture as a warning, affirmation, or correction.
- If the enemy tries to mislead us with Scripture (he does this; we'll talk about this more in the next lesson), the Holy Spirit will help us discern truth.
- He may bring verses to mind to pray for a situation or person.
- He may teach us something about God's ways as we read and hear Scriptures over a period of time.
- He might bring light to passages of Scripture that confuse us.

6. Another way the Holy Spirit comes alongside is when we need to act in a situation about which God's written Word is not specific. Following are two scenarios. Read the Scriptures that go with each and state as definitively as you can your understanding of God's will for that situation.

a. Someone has offended you. Consider Proverbs 19:11 and Matthew 18:15. What does Scripture say you should do?

b. A widower is thinking of getting remarried. Consider Proverbs 18:22 and 1 Corinthians 7:1, 8. Would God want him to do this?

Okay, I admit it—those were trick questions. And the point here is not to debate or try to settle which action is the "right" one. In fact, I don't even want us to attempt to! What I want us to see is how much we need the Holy Spirit to interpret for us in these kinds of situations. If we try to apply our own understanding, we can end up in knots.

But hopefully you can see from them how we need more than just the written word plus our own understanding to navigate questions like these. If I were facing these questions (and I have faced such questions!), I would be entering into dialogue with God, through the Holy Spirit, about my situation and the Scriptures that seem to address it. I would definitely be seeking God for specific, personal input and guidance—and I'd be careful not to move forward until I was pretty sure I'd heard clearly from Him!

RECEIVE THE HOLY SPIRIT'S HELP

Have you ever wondered why God chose the dove to represent the Holy Spirit? Why a dove and not, say, a blue jay? I'm only guessing here, but I think it might be because the blue jay is bold, loud, and aggressive. And *pushy*! When I haven't responded to their persistent demands for handouts, I've had jays rob me nearly blind right at my very own picnic table.

The dove, on the other hand, is a gentle bird, easily chased away. In some ways, the Holy Spirit is like that, I think. He is meek, not pushy. He does not force. He will quietly interrupt us to lead, warn, teach, or encourage, but if we don't respond to Him, if we're too occupied with bustle and noise, if we brush Him off or resist Him, He's likely to back off and leave us alone—at least for a while. For that reason, it's important that we intentionally cultivate our relationship with the Holy Spirit. And so we need to learn how to live by the Spirit and keep in step with Him (see Galatians 5:25).

1. In what ways do you think the Holy Spirit's help could be stifled, or blocked? See Jeremiah 6:10; Acts 7:51; Ephesians 4:30; 1 Thessalonians 5:18-20; James 1:6.

2. Are any of these getting in your way of receiving His help? Confess them and ask Him to transform your heart so that you can enjoy clear, unobstructed conversation with God through His Word (and in other ways, too!).

3. In this lesson, we've seen many ways the Holy Spirit initiates and interprets for us as we read the Bible and talk with God. Which of these ways would you like to become more aware of as you relate with God?

YOUR TURN

This week you will have an opportunity to practice inviting the Holy Spirit to interpret Scripture for you and to initiate speaking to you through it (or perhaps through other means). Conversation with the Holy Spirit *is* prayer, it's just not praying through a list and asking God for what you and your loved ones need.

For each of the next two days choose one of the passages suggested below to read in the meditative manner you used in the "Invite God to Speak" section of this lesson. (Review the instructions there if you need a refresher.) Following each set of references is a space for you to write your reflections (His personal interpretation of the passage to you) and also places to note any initiating He may do and your prayer responses to Him.

Keep in mind that His initiating could take place during your quiet time but it is equally likely to occur at other times throughout the day (or night) so stay alert to the possibility of Him interrupting you. Also realize that He may initiate/interrupt with Scriptures besides the one you are spending time with that day. And if you don't notice any initiating, that's fine, too.

Before you read each time, invite the Holy Spirit to speak to you. And as you finish your time with Him, thank Him for whatever He shared and invite Him to continue speaking to you throughout your day.

PSALM 23

What do you sense the Holy Spirit saying to you personally through this passage?

How did He initiate with you today?

What would you like to say to God about the things He is saying to you?

LUKE 15:11-31

What do you sense the Holy Spirit saying to you personally through this passage?

How did He initiate with you today?

What would you like to say to God about the things He is saying to you?

JOHN 8:1-11

What do you sense the Holy Spirit saying to you personally through this passage?

How did He initiate with you today?

What would you like to say to God about the things He is saying to you?

ROMANS 8:28-39

What do you sense the Holy Spirit saying to you personally through this passage?

How did He initiate with you today?

What would you like to say to God about the things He is saying to you?

"Did I Hear You Right?"

YEARS AGO, I WAS UNCERTAIN about whether God would speak to me personally—as Friend to friend, Father to daughter, specifically about the subjective details of my life. So I asked, tentatively, hopefully, but not with a lot of confidence. However, not long after I began asking Him to speak to me, I noticed that Scripture passages started jumping off the pages at me. There were lots of them, but two in particular really got me: "Call to me and I will answer you and tell you great and unsearchable things you do not know" (Jeremiah 33:3), and "My sheep listen to my voice; I know them, and they follow me" (John 10:27).

The way this happened was like a conversation between Him and me. The summary version went kind of like this:

- *God (subtly hinting, so I didn't even know it was Him—I thought it was my own thoughts):* Wouldn't it be nice if you could hear Me talk to you the same way your friends and family talk to you?
- *Me (after hearing these suggestions over months or even years, thinking they were my own great idea):* God, I'd really like it if I could talk to You like a good friend. I know You're supposed to be my best friend, but how can I have a deep relationship with You if You don't talk to me? Would You really talk to me?
- *God (through various Scriptures):* Yes, see? Here it says in My Word that I really will talk to you!
- *Me (convinced because I read it in His written Word):* Okay, then,

God, You say that You want to speak to me, that You will answer me when I call to You, that Your sheep (and I *am* one of Your sheep) listen to Your voice. So, God, please talk to me!

And, after having several conversations like this, I started to hear God speak to me! Over time, He taught me to listen to His voice and grow in my ability to hear from Him.

THINK ABOUT IT

Learning to distinguish God's voice from other messages we might receive is what we call spiritual discernment. Why is discernment such an important skill to have when we enter into two-way conversational prayer with God?

INVITE GOD TO SPEAK

If we are to hear the Holy Spirit and receive life as He opens up Scripture to us, we must develop ears that hear Him accurately and truly. Our flesh, the enemy, and even religious tradition can misuse Scripture with us in ways that block this life-giving dialogue. The Apostle Paul said of the church at Corinth, "But I am afraid that just as Eve was deceived by the serpent's cunning, your minds may somehow be led astray from your sincere and pure devotion to Christ" (2 Corinthians 11:3). We, too, want to guard our minds so that we are not led astray from Christ.

1. Prayer often needs to be both defensive and offensive. We pray *for* God's purposes and *against* the enemy's. You can use 2 Corinthians 11:3 to pray this kind of double-edged prayer:

a. What can you pray *for* from this verse?

b. What should you pray protection *against?*

2. Write a prayer below that covers both of these elements. Use this prayer, or one like it, as you ask God to help you stay clear of the enemy's deception so that you can hear His voice clearly and confidently, without confusion.

GOING DEEPER

Before I began to relate closely with God and receive His word as we have talked about, I was often undiscerning. I was not open to hearing God outside of Scripture because I didn't want to be deceived, but at the same time, I didn't recognize that my ability to hear God clearly through the Bible could be clouded and distorted. Without realizing it, I came to believe that any Scripture that came to me in any way—whether through my reading, through another person, or through my own thoughts—was

God speaking literally and directly to me. I had no grid for understanding that people, my own thoughts, and even the enemy could speak Scripture to me in ways that twisted what God intended.

For example, when I was a little girl, the window blinds in my room were difficult for me to manage. Rather than fuss with them, I often left them down, even when it was noon and the sun was shining. But one day I was jolted by a Scripture that I noticed for the first time: "Men loved darkness rather than light because their deeds were evil!" (John 3:19, KJV). A dagger of shame penetrated my tender heart with those words. Because I knew they were Scripture, I took them to heart and felt that God was condemning me. Yet that was *not* God's personal word to me, a little girl who simply had trouble operating window blinds. Whether it was the enemy or simply my own thoughts, it was *not* God who was speaking to me.

Years later, as a young adult, I read about the unpardonable sin (Matthew 12:31-32). Although I did not understand what that sin was, the moment I read about it, I was sure I'd committed it. Fear gripped me to the extent that I could not sleep night after night. Finally I got counsel from another believer who helped me understand that God had not been addressing me through that verse and I had not committed that sin. I've learned since then that my experience with that passage is not unusual.

I'm glad to say that as God has taught me more about how He speaks—and doesn't speak—I am not so frequently messed up by encounters like these with God's Word.

This lesson is intended to help you think through the ways we can sometimes make harmful mistakes in the way we hear God through His written Word—and why talking to God about what we hear is so important.

The master deceiver, our enemy, Satan, masquerades as an angel of light (2 Corinthians 11:14) and prowls around looking for people to devour (1 Peter 5:8). For those of us who love the Lord and His written

Word, one of the prime methods the enemy uses to try to deceive us is by twisting the words of Scripture. Because we don't want to stop listening to God, we must instead pray for and learn spiritual discernment so we can be confident that what we hear is truly from God.

1. Read each of the following passages. For each, write a summary of how God's words were being misused. Consider these aspects: What passages or words from God were being used? Were they quoted directly or implied? Were they misquoted or twisted, and if so, how? What was at risk?

    a. Genesis 2:15-17; 3:1-2

    b. Matthew 4:5-7 (with Psalm 91:11-12; Deuteronomy 6:16)

    c. Luke 13:10-16 (with Exodus 20:8-11)

    d. John 12:1-8 (with Proverbs 19:17; 28:27)

DEVELOPING DISCERNMENT

How do we avoid being deceived by the inappropriate application of Scripture—or by any word that we think *could* be a word from God? There are several points to remember.

• The Holy Spirit will deepen our trust in and love for God.

The enemy is all about trying to **make God look bad** so that we will be reluctant to trust Him and afraid to draw near to Him. This is his oldest trick. If you hear a Scripture that seems to put God in a bad light, proceed with extreme caution.

Example: Matthew 5:48, "Be perfect, therefore, as your heavenly Father is perfect," was a verse that used to cause me major God-avoidance issues in my young adult years. When I heard that verse, I conjured up an image of a strict schoolteacher or capricious cop who was just waiting to catch me slip up. I knew I wasn't perfect! But the idea that God expected me to be put Him in a bad light for me. I had no idea how to draw near to a God like that. So, very often I didn't even try. "Just fly under the radar" seemed like a safer strategy than getting the notice of a perfectionistic God like that.

• The Holy Spirit will never condemn us (see Romans 8:1, 33-34). When He corrects us, He does it in a way that holds out life and hope.

The enemy, on the other hand, is all about **making us look and feel bad** and think we are beyond hope or help. In Revelation 12:10 he is called "the accuser." Sometimes he quotes Scripture to us about things that are actually true—for instance, ways we have sinned—but he does it in a way that insinuates shame, judgment, and futility.

Example: Recently I spoke with a troubled friend and too quickly offered words that, though true, were not helpful to her. Though I was trying to support her, I actually made her feel worse. Immediately my rapid-fire thoughts threw Scripture at me. "Will you *ever* remember that you are only supposed to speak 'that which is good to the use of edifying, that it may minister grace unto the hearers' (Ephesians 4:29, KJV). You know you're supposed to 'be quick to listen' and 'slow to speak' (James 1:19). But your tongue is 'a fire, a world of evil!' (James 3:6). And now you've offended your friend. You'll never win her back because 'an offended brother is more unyielding than a fortified city' (Proverbs 18:19)."

Although the Scriptures that came at me were true, I knew this was not the Holy Spirit because His purpose is never to condemn and defeat me. God would *never* correct me that way!

- The Holy Spirit will lead us into truth.

    The enemy **lifts verses out of context** to imply something different than what the whole of Scripture really says.

    Example: Maturing as a Christian means inviting the Lord into different areas of sin and struggle. At any given stage of my life with God, He is usually working with me to help me overcome some sin pattern that keeps me from experiencing His life. Even though my Father is patient and gentle with me, during these times of soul-searching and growth, inevitably the enemy will beat me up with 1 John 3:9: "No one who is born of God will continue to sin, because God's seed remains in him; he cannot go on sinning, because he has been born of God." As a young adult, that single verse—taken alone, without the context of the rest of Scripture—would do a number on me, sometimes even causing me to doubt whether I even belonged to God. I'm wiser to the enemy now, but he still tries to take me out with that Scripture and ones like it.

- The Holy Spirit builds us up and helps us to build up others, too.

    The enemy tries to deceive us by **using Scripture to justify**

sin: neglect of or harshness toward others, crossing moral lines, failing to do good, etc.

Example: My mother-in-law was a nineteen-year-old newly-wed during the Great Depression. She and her young husband lived with his parents to save money. Every day she searched for work, but employment was difficult to find for anyone, much less for an unskilled immigrant who was just learning English. When evening came and it was time for her to sit down with her husband's family for dinner, her father-in-law would often quote 2 Thessalonians 3:10 to her: "If any would not work, neither should he eat." He didn't actually deny her the meal—but can you imagine what she felt each time she heard that? And how the memory of those words wounded her for years to come?

1. Can you think of a personal example of a time when you were deceived by the misuse of Scripture? What happened? If you wanted to counsel someone else so they could avoid a similar experience, what would you suggest?

2. What have you learned in this lesson or from other experiences, that could help you grow in discernment?

YOUR TURN

Choose two of the following prayer exercises to help you experience these truths through relational conversation with God.

EXERCISE 1:

What thoughts have come to you as you've done this lesson? Has Scripture ever come to you in a distorted, unhelpful way? Is any of that distortion still active—that is, do you currently find yourself struggling with confusion, condemnation, hesitancy toward God, or other effects because certain Scriptures have taken on non-life-giving meaning for you? If so, dialogue with God about it.

- ☐ Tell Him what you are feeling and thinking.
- ☐ Ask Him to silence the enemy so that you only hear God's voice.
- ☐ Then ask Him to show you what is true. Ask Him to give you Scriptures that bring balance to the one that is being twisted for you.
- ☐ Respond to what He shows you—is the matter cleared up for you? Thank Him! Tell Him how you think this will affect your life and relationships. Do you still have questions? Ask them and keep the conversation going. Are you stuck? Ask Him if there's someone He would like you to talk to about your questions, then follow through with what He says.

EXERCISE 2:

Do certain Scriptures stir a fearful, resentful, despairing, or other negative response in you? Write down the references for as many as you can recall. Pick one of these passages and pray through it according to the following guidelines.

☐ Tell God (or Jesus) how what you read makes you feel.

☐ Ask Him any questions the passage raises for you.

☐ Now ask Him to respond to your questions and feelings. You could say something simple like, "Jesus, would You please talk to me about the things I am experiencing in this passage?" You might continue with something like "What do You want me to understand about myself or about You based on what You are saying to me through these verses?" Write down what you sense He might be saying to you.

☐ Respond to Him. If He has encouraged you, thank Him for that and tell Him how you feel encouraged. If you are uncomfortable or experiencing other difficult emotions, talk to Him about them. Be honest. Expect Him to help you with whatever you are struggling with and write down what you think He might be saying. If you still feel stuck, get a mature Christian friend to pray and listen to God with you.

EXERCISE 3:

Prevention is always the best medicine. When it comes to safeguarding yourself from the enemy's traps, the best thing you can do is to focus on Jesus. Think back to 2 Corinthians 11:3 that we looked at earlier in this lesson: "But I am afraid that just as Eve was deceived by the serpent's cunning, your minds may somehow be led astray from your sincere and pure devotion to Christ." If you stand firm in your "sincere and pure devotion to Christ" it's going to be pretty hard for the enemy to take you out.

☐ Reflect with God for a bit on this question: "What do You want me to realize and remember about You, Your character, Your ways, Your thoughts and feelings about me (etc.) so that my devotion to Jesus will grow even deeper, more sincere, and more pure?"

☐ Meditate on John 10, Philippians 2, or some other passage that reveals God's character, heart, and ways.

☐ Write down what you sense Him saying. Ask Him for Scriptures to support the things He shares with you. Then meditate on these Scriptures for the rest of this week (or even longer).

EXERCISE 4:

Perhaps you have inadvertently used Scripture in a way that did not bring life to someone else. Maybe you too easily shared a Bible verse, meaning to encourage someone, when the person just wasn't ready to hear it. Or maybe you quoted Scripture to someone, trying to help them make a good decision, but in so doing, you aborted their efforts to hear from God for themselves. Talk to God about this. Confess what you did and its effects on the other person. Ask God's forgiveness. Ask Him if He would like you to seek the forgiveness of the other person as well (and follow through if He says to).

Keep in mind that though Jesus was very aware of people's sins and shortcomings, He didn't always respond to them with Scripture. (If you're interested in studying this, read Mark 10:35-40; Luke 22:43-62; John 8:1-11. For each situation consider what Jesus could have said and what Scriptures He could have quoted, then reflect on what He did instead.)

Read (and perhaps memorize) Ephesians 4:29: "Let everything you say be good and helpful, so that your words will be an encouragement to those who hear them" (NLT). Then ask God to help your conversations—including ones where you refer (either explicitly or implicitly) to His word—to be useful to build up those you speak with. Practice praying like this before meetings, phone calls, writing emails, conversations with friends and family, and so on.

Borrowed Prayers, Part 1

EARLY IN OUR MARRIAGE, my late husband and I visited a church that used written prayers—many of them closely adapted from Scripture. We had mixed reactions to the experience because of our different prayer backgrounds. To me, the prayers were deeply meaningful. They were beautiful and rich and expressed my heart in ways that I wouldn't have thought to on my own. My husband, on the other hand, struggled to keep his mind from wandering. The words didn't connect for him.

Our different responses stemmed from our backgrounds. My husband had been raised in a religious culture that never prayed spontaneous prayers; the only prayers he ever heard or prayed were written or recited prayers. Somewhere along the line, he had just learned to tune them out. Learning to pray in his own words had been liberating for him.

Conversely, the religious tradition I was raised in encouraged spontaneous prayers and for the most part discouraged praying others' prayers. There seemed to be a general understanding that reading or reciting previously prayed prayers amounted to "rote" praying—our congregation didn't even regularly pray the familiar Lord's Prayer given by Jesus. So the idea of borrowing others' prayers was new and meaningful to me.

THINK ABOUT IT

1. Have your traditions and experiences caused you to have a bias toward or against praying others' prayers?

2. What benefits do you see from

praying in your own words?

praying written prayers?

3. Can you think of drawbacks to either kind of praying?

4. If your praying already includes written prayers, share some of the ones that have been most meaningful to you.

INVITE GOD TO SPEAK

Regardless of your tradition, at some point you have probably prayed the Lord's Prayer from Matthew 6:9-13:

Our Father in heaven, hallowed be your name,

your kingdom come, your will be done on earth as it is in
heaven.
Give us today our daily bread.
Forgive us our debts, as we also have forgiven our debtors.
And lead us not into temptation, but deliver us from the
evil one.

I believe Jesus gave us the Lord's Prayer to use as a model. We can read
or recite it "as is"—and as long as our minds and hearts are engaged,
that's a very good thing to do. Or we can use it as a prayer outline. For
example, instead of praying for "daily bread" you might ask God for
other needs such as a job or rent money or healing from an illness.

Another way to pray it is to pray it with the help of the Holy Spirit,
inviting Him to personalize it for you according to the opportunities
and challenges of any given day—things He happens to know more
about than we do! Try praying the Lord's Prayer in this manner, inviting God to speak into the prayer and make it personal for you.

- To try this, pray the prayer a section at a time (dividing the
  prayer however you like). If your first topic includes "Our Father in heaven, hallowed be your name," pause there to talk
  with God. Ask Him questions. You might ask Him what He
  wants you to know about His parenting of you this day. Or
  you might ask Him what part of His character He'd like you
  to focus on in praise. Perhaps you could ask Him how you can
  participate in making His name holy in your world this day.
- After you ask Him your question, be still and quiet for a while
  and listen for His response. Write down the impressions that
  come to you. Maybe He will say He wants you to know that He
  is not only your Father, but also your son or daughter's Father,
  and that you can trust Him to work in his or her life today. Per-

haps He will tell you that He wants to be worshiped as *faithful* today, that He wants you to know how trustworthy He is so you can really depend on Him.

- Pray through the prayer in this manner, asking God questions after each section, and then waiting for His responses. Write down what you think you hear Him saying. Then pray these things back to Him.

- After you've prayed this way, jot down some notes about your experience. What did God show you when you asked Him to help you pray the prayer? Did He surprise you? Did you notice Him answering those prayers throughout the day? Did this practice encourage or enhance your conversations with Him in any way?

GOING DEEPER

In the past few lessons, we've seen how God uses His written Word to bring life to our prayers. When the Holy Spirit interrupts and initiates with us, He brings God's words alive. In the next lessons, we'll begin to look at specific ways we can use God's written Word to talk with Him.

The Bible is full of prayers, some of them familiar to us, others less so. It provides prayers we can borrow for nearly anything we might want to pray about. When we open the Bible with the intent to grow in our relationship and conversation with God, His Spirit leads us to discover all kinds of wonderful things. We see God's invitation to pray about subjects that may never otherwise have made it into our conversations with Him. We find words that express our hearts better than we can on our own—and companionship with pray-ers throughout history who have shared similar feelings as ours and provided examples of how to express them to God.

EXPANDING OUR PRAYERS

1. A few years ago, Bruce Wilkerson wrote a best-selling book about three little verses in the Bible that give us the prayer of someone almost nobody had paid much attention to up until that point. Read 1 Chronicles 4:9-10 and write down what Jabez, the person mentioned there, prayed.

Some people criticized the book, and by association, Jabez's prayer itself, which they found to be self-centered. However, God doesn't condemn Jabez—in fact, He answered that prayer. So I decided that God must have been okay with Jabez's prayer, so I would be, too. I don't know that I had ever thought to ask God to "enlarge my territory" before—but with Jabez's example and the Holy Spirit's invitation, I started doing so. And guess what, God has answered my prayer, too, expanding my ministry in both numbers and reach.

2. Read the Scriptures that follow and notice some of the other things God's Word suggests we can (or perhaps even should) talk to Him about. Summarize each.

a. Genesis 32:24-28

b. 2 Kings 6:15-17

c. Psalm 122:4-9

d. Psalm 139:23-24

e. Proverbs 30:7-9

f. Luke 6:28

3. Which of these topics, generally speaking, are part of your typical conversations with God?

4. Are there any topics here that intrigue you that you might want to talk with God about more often? Which ones?

PROVIDING WORDS WHEN ORDINARY WORDS FAIL

There have been several seasons in my life when it was hard for me to pray. My heart was so overwhelmed—sometimes with joy, sometimes with pain—that I couldn't find my own voice to talk with God. During these times the Holy Spirit has led me to prayers that help express what I cannot. These prayers become anchors for me. Here are some of the prayers that have especially been meaningful to me. Read them and after each write the type of situation these prayers might provide words for.

I could use this when . . .

a. Psalm 8

b. Psalm 23

c. Psalm 27:7-14

d. Psalm 51

e. Psalm 73:25-26

f. Mark 9:24

g. Luke 18:38

Next time words fail you, don't stop praying. Revisit these Scripture prayers and borrow words from someone else.

YOUR TURN

Review this lesson. Which verses and ideas caught your interest?

Is there one you'd like to pray every day for the rest of this week? Or several that you would like to pray on different days or throughout the day? Write down which one(s) you selected. Then try them out and jot down what your experiences with them were like.

Borrowed Prayers, Part 2

SOME TIME AGO, I WAS struggling to love some difficult people. It seemed that whatever I did backfired. I had talked to God about it *a lot*—but hadn't gotten any clear direction. Then one day when I opened my Bible to the bookmarked place, God's very personal Word came to me in the form of a prayer I'd never noticed before. "And it is my prayer that your love may abound more and more, with knowledge and all discernment" (Philippians 1:9, esv).

Love *and discernment*. That was what I had been missing. I'd been trying to love, but had not been seeking God's discernment for how best to do that. He knew better than I did—better, even, than the people themselves—how they needed to be loved.

On my own, I never would have thought to pray like that—but I knew it was God's gracious direction. So I prayed that prayer for a few weeks and, incredibly to me (since I'd been praying and struggling and stuck for so long) things shifted in the relationship and my love started to be genuinely received. How cool is that?

THINK ABOUT IT

Can you think of a new-to-you type of praying that you learned about in the Bible? What was it? What happened when you started praying that way?

INVITE GOD TO SPEAK

The Bible enlarges our concepts of prayer, giving us ideas and words to pray that we might never come up with on our own. This week, use Psalm 119:18, a prayer of David, as a way of inviting God to show you new things that will enrich your conversations with Him: "Open my eyes that I may see wonderful things in your law." Pray this prayer each day as you begin working on your lesson. Feel free to personalize it according to what you need and are feeling on a given day; for example, you might choose one of the following "add-ons" to make this prayer your own:

- I haven't been hearing much that has meant anything personally to me lately, God. Please open my eyes that I may see wonderful things in Your Law.
- I wish I saw more "wonderful" things in Your words and fewer things that discourage me, Lord. Won't You open my eyes that I may see *wonderful* things in Your Law?
- I've been amazed at the incredible ways You've spoken to me through the Bible lately, Father. Will You open my eyes today so that I may see even more wonderful things in Your Law?

GOING DEEPER

In the last lesson we saw how God can use His written Word to show us new ways to pray and new topics to pray about. This week we'll look at how seeing what He has recorded for us gives us permission to express our hearts to God in ways we may not have realized we could, and also how it inspires us to pray with faith we might not ordinarily come up with on our own.

PERMITTING US TO EXPRESS OUR NEGATIVE EMOTIONS

Although I'd read the Bible from cover to cover a number of times, it wasn't until I was going through an extended time of deep pain and confusion that I noticed just how gritty and honest some of the prayers in there are. Read or skim the following prayers for yourself, and I think you'll see what I mean.

- Job 10

- Psalm 88

- Jeremiah 20:7-18

- Matthew 27:46

1. Why do you suppose the Holy Spirit included these prayers in God's written Word?

2. Did you find any parts of these prayers unusual or surprising? If so, which parts and why?

3. If you were deeply feeling pain, confusion, anger, depression, or fear like these pray-ers apparently were, would you be able to pray in a similarly honest way? Why or why not?

4. How could praying like this affect your relationship with God? Do you think you would become closer to Him?

The first time I got gut-level honest with God and prayed what I was actually thinking and feeling, I wondered if lightning might strike me. But it didn't! Instead, I sensed God drawing near to me, understanding my pain, having compassion on me. "The LORD is near to the brokenhearted and saves the crushed in spirit," David tells us in Psalm 34:18, and that is what I experienced. But as long as I held my emotions tight inside me, pretending I was all right, trying to act and pray the way I thought "good Christians" did, I had kept Him out. I didn't sense Him come close until I got really honest and admitted what was really going on inside me—something He already knew. If it weren't for Scripture prayers like the ones you read in this section (and many more like them throughout the Bible), I might have never dared to pray in total honesty—and I may have never sensed God's deep compassion for me.

INSPIRING US TO HIGH-ROAD PRAYING

1. When I sense impending disaster, my praying can sometimes sound more like panicking-aloud-to-God than actual prayer. I'm still talking to God, and that's far better than avoiding Him or trying to find my own solution. However, certain Scriptures inspire me to pray with more trust, confidence, and hope. Read the following passages. After each one, write down what the crisis was and how the pray-er(s) talked to God about it.

      a. Psalm 3 (read with note introducing the Psalm; for more background about David and Absalom, read 2 Samuel 15)

      b. 2 Chronicles 20:1-12

      c. Acts 4:12-31

2. What themes do you notice in these prayers?

3. How does this compare with how you might ordinarily pray in these situations?

4. How do these themes inspire you to pray more "high-road" prayers?

5. How has this lesson encouraged, equipped, inspired, or challenged you?

Philippians 4:6-7 is a passage familiar to many Christians, especially believers who care a lot about prayer: "Do not be anxious about anything, but in every situation, by prayer and petition, with thanksgiving, present your requests to God. And the peace of God, which transcends all understanding, will guard your hearts and your minds in Christ Jesus." So when the Holy Spirit brought that passage to mind recently, I thought He was just reminding me not to worry so much and to pray more about the situations that were causing me anxiety.

However, a phrase stuck out to me as I pondered those familiar words: *with thanksgiving*. Ordinarily, I've usually breezed right over that part of the instruction. If you'd ask me God's method for having peace that passes understanding I probably would have said, "Don't worry, but pray about everything." And I would have been half right. Yes, God definitely wants me to give Him my worries and heartaches, my frustrations and fears—but He wants me to mingle those with thanksgiving.

So I tried it. I thought about all my piles at work and my deadlines. I prayed and asked God for wisdom and help to get it done—well and on time. And then I took it the next step and thanked Him for the excellent team I work with who make the workload lighter and a whole lot more fun. *Hmmm. I feel more peaceful already.*

I thought about a big decision I had to make that felt really hard to me. I used to make big decisions with my husband and even though he'd been gone five years already, I still missed him. So I prayed and asked God for guidance to make the decision. To lead me into His paths. And then I thanked Him for all the ways He had faithfully guided me since my husband's death. He really has been a Husband to me. He hasn't failed me yet—I don't think He will this time, either. My heart was able to rest.

The Holy Spirit's gentle invitation to ponder more deeply a familiar passage of Scripture enabled me to pray prayers that were more "high road" than I would have ordinarily prayed. And the result for me was peace.

YOUR TURN

Pick one Scripture passage from each of the two sections in this lesson ("Permitting Us to Express Our Negative Emotions" and "Inspiring Us to High-Road Praying"). Pray that passage as your own prayer, or use it as a guideline for praying your own similar prayer. Jot notes about each prayer experience below.

The first passage I selected:

_____.

My experience with praying it:

The second passage I selected:

_____.

My experience with praying it:

Beyond Prayer Formulas

ONE OF THE MOST OBVIOUS benefits of praying with the help of Scripture is knowing that we are praying for the things God wants. This lends confidence and hope to our praying. And when we pray with God *relationally*, in dialogue with Him as our loving Father and intimate Friend, we are not so tempted to approach prayer as a formula: "If I pray the right things in the right way, I will get the result I expect."

With these ideas in mind, very often my prayers go through a process. I start by letting God know my desires, needs, dreams, and hopes—but I hold them loosely. While continuing to pray these loosely held prayers, I ask Him to tell me what He has in mind. The most common way He reveals this to me is through His written Word. I might read the Bible and something jumps off the page at me, or His Spirit might remind me of a certain verse or passage, or sometimes I come across it in a sermon, song, conversation, book, or article (all of these are ways He speaks to me). Once I have a verse or passage that seems to indicate God's heart for my situation, I will change the way I pray to something a bit bolder: *God, You say in Your Word that _____ so I'm asking You to _____. Would You please say more to me about what You want in this situation so I can get on board with You?*

It's really quite similar to how most of us go about making requests of friends and family. Don't you make your requests based on what you know about the person? If you know your friend actually enjoys using his pickup truck to help people move, then you can feel pretty confident asking him to bring his truck for a Saturday and help you move, right? In relationships where you know someone well, you can feel freedom and assurance that your requests of that person will receive good answers—because you make requests according to who that person is, what he or she values, what he or she has power and resources to do.

It's far from a perfect analogy, but it may help us understand a little of what happens with God. If it's relationship we are seeking with God, we will not use His written Word in order to find the magic words that will obligate Him to do what we want Him to. Instead, we get to know Him—what He's like, what He wants, what He likes and doesn't like. And out of relationship with Him, as a Person whom we love, enjoy, and respect, we will ask Him for what we need and want. Of course, one of the chief ways we get to know these things about God is through what He inspired to be written about Himself in the Bible and through our conversations with Him.

THINK ABOUT IT

Can you think of a time you prayed or "claimed" a specific promise from the Bible? What did you pray for? What Scripture(s) did you use to back up your request? How did the situation you prayed about turn out? How did that experience affect your feelings about God and your relationship with Him?

INVITE GOD TO SPEAK

1. What are you praying about right now? List one or two prayer concerns.

2. What has God said or told you about Himself in His Word that gives you direction and confidence as you pray about this matter? If you already know, write it below.

3. If you don't know yet, ask the Holy Spirit to bring to mind Scriptures that apply to your situation(s). If you don't hear anything right away, keep praying, and keep asking Him to speak to you through His Word about what you are talking with Him about.

4. When you get a fairly clear idea of what God is saying to you from His Word about your request, adjust your request as needed so that it lines up with what He wants for you.

5. Write a prayer below that reflects both God's desire and yours for the concern you are talking with Him about. Pray this prayer each day, and keep listening for anything else God wants to say to you along the way.

GOING DEEPER

1. In John 14, Jesus says, "I will do whatever you ask in my name, so that the Son may bring glory to the Father. You may ask me for anything in my name, and I will do it" (verses 13-14). That's an amazing promise. And this isn't the only verse like this in Scripture. Over and over we see promises that God will answer prayers when we remain in Him, agree with two or three people, ask in His name, have faith, don't waver (e.g. Matthew 18:19; John 14:13-14; 15:7; James 1:5-8; 5:14-16; 1 John 3:21-22; 5:14-15). How do those promises compare with your experiences with prayer?

If you're like me, you've probably had some wonderful experiences when God did answer those prayers and you were amazed. But, like me, you may also have had experiences where what you've asked God to do is not what He has done—at least not from your perspective.

So what do we do with that? I don't think there are any easy answers to that question. However, for my part, as I have invited God to speak to me about my situations I often have learned things about His timing and His nature that have encouraged me to continue to pray and trust Him. He has shown me two factors that may be in play when my requests aren't answered the way Scripture seems to say they should be. The first factor is timing, and the second is the larger picture of what's going on.

ALL IN GOOD TIME

1. Read the following Scriptures. Although they are not all specifical-

ly about God's promises, the principles still apply. What do you learn about trusting God and waiting on Him from these verses?

    a. Habakkuk 2:3

    b. Luke 18:1-8

    c. 2 Peter 3:9

    d. Hebrews 11

2. How do these verses help you, as you consider promises you have been praying for a long time?

It helped me to understand that when God isn't answering my prayers as it seems He should, timing might be a factor. Despite the firm belief most of us have in eternal life, for many of us what we call "life" here on earth, practically amounts to about eighty years, give or take a few. We rarely think about the life we have with God that continues—without skipping a beat—long after we take our final breaths here on earth. I can be pretty impatient; I don't like to concede that in His view, one of His days is like a thousand of mine (2 Peter 3:8).

    We see this play out in different ways. Abraham, to give a well-known example, was given the promise of offspring at the ripe old age of seventy-five (Genesis 12:7). By all accounts, it would seem logical that such a promise would come to pass quickly, since he was already old and Sarah, at sixty-five, was no spring chicken, either. However, God did not fulfill His promise to Abraham and Sarah for many years—twenty-five years, in fact. Would I have kept praying and believing that long? I'm not so sure.

Like them, for some of us, the promises will take years or even decades to come. For others of us, however, they might not come until the other side of eternity. Yet, I am confident those of us who pray God's promises with faith will see the healing, salvation, reconciliation, and restoration we have prayed for on the other side of death, even if not before.

Along with being aware that God's timing may be different from ours, another factor is often in play when we ask God to work: Many times our prayers aren't just about us—they depend on God's larger plans and on the actions of others.

IT'S NOT (ONLY) ABOUT YOU

Something that I had to understand was that many of our prayers involve more than just us. Sometimes there could be dark forces slowing things down, as in the well-known example in Daniel 10:12-14. Other times the delay may have human causes. If we pray for revival, the return of a wayward friend or family member, the restoration of a relationship, or justice for oppressed people—just to name a few examples—we are really hoping that people will repent or take certain actions. Even though our prayers may be very clearly in God's will, God highly values human free will. Jesus never forced anyone to do anything. He invited them to follow Him and experience life. However, many people did not then (and do not now) yield to His invitations or warnings. God does not make people do things they do not want to do.

1. When you take into account that other people and God's bigger

picture may be involved in the good and right things for which you are praying, how might that affect the way you pray?

(**Hint:** Focus your prayers at what God can do in the situation rather than just on what you want the person or people to do. For example, you might ask the Holy Spirit to remind a person of the truth she knew as a child. Or you might ask God to surround a person with godly and wise advisors who will point him to truth.)

Though it has been helpful for me to be aware of God's timing and the other people who might be involved in my prayers, the primary thing that has helped me when I am puzzled about praying according to God's promises is to remember that prayer isn't about using a formula to get the exact results I want. Prayer is about *relationship*.

IT'S ABOUT RELATIONSHIP

As we've seen throughout this study, prayer is about relating with God. He reveals Himself to us in His written Word and tells us how life with Him works. But that doesn't mean we can treat what we see in the Bible as a formula that, if we get it exactly right, obligates God to do exactly what we are asking.

1. Read 2 Corinthians 12:7-10 and notice the conversation that took

place between Paul and God. On what basis do you think Paul made his request (that is, do you think he asked according to God's character, word, or will)? How long did he pray for what he wanted? Did Paul get what he asked for? What might have happened if he had stopped praying instead of persevering as he did? How do you suppose his relationship with God deepened as a result of this extended exchange?

Paul prayed fervently, more than once, yet didn't receive what he asked for. However, what he did receive was a new perspective, one that was deeply satisfying to him. He began understanding and relating with God in a whole new way as a result.

The more I grow in my relationship with God, viewing prayer in the context of loving conversation with my good, wise, and loving Friend, I'm finding that I'm not as put out when my prayers aren't answered in the fashion I hope they will be. These days, unanswered prayer becomes a topic for lively ongoing conversation with God. I don't just drop my request in the Celestial Suggestion Box and wait for something to happen. Now I'm more likely to have a running conversation about whatever it is I'm asking God to do.

Here are some of the questions I might ask Him to talk with me about:

- What do You see about this situation that I can't, God? What are You doing behind the scenes?
- How are You working to transform me in this situation, God?
- How should I be praying concerning the other people involved in this situation?
- How might You want me to partner with You for the answer to this need?
- Am I getting in Your way somehow? Will You show me anything in me that hinders You from answering?
- Should I be asking You for something different, God? Maybe I'm asking the wrong thing?
- What would You like for me to be doing while I wait for You to come through on this, Father?
- What would You like me to better understand about You and Your character as I wait on You for this need or desire, God?

YOUR TURN

EXERCISE 1: Getting God's Perspective

List three to five things you are thinking about. These should be things that are important to you and that you would like to pray about (or are already praying about). These can be about anything—for example, wisdom about what college your son or daughter should go to, whether you should agree to participate in a certain ministry, how you would like to see growth in a particular relationship, a health need, etc.

1.

2.

3.

4.

5.

Over the next few days, pick one of these prayer requests each day to focus on. Then, take the following steps to help you get God's perspective about your prayer topic so that you can become confident that what you are asking lines up with His desires (or you can adjust if it doesn't). Isaiah 55:8-9 is a wonderful Scripture to pray as you work through this process: "'For my thoughts are not your thoughts, neither are your ways my ways,' declares the Lord. 'As the heavens are higher than the earth, so are my ways higher than your ways and my thoughts than your thoughts.'"

- Pray the verses aloud. Change the pronouns so that you are addressing God "For *your* thoughts are not *my* thoughts" (and so on) and simply say it to God slowly, thoughtfully, worshipfully. Let your heart and mind engage with the words as you think about who He is and who you are to Him.

- Pray the verse again, only this time personalize it by inserting your concern into the appropriate part of the verse. For example, "For your thoughts <u>about where Emily should go to college</u> are not my thoughts, neither are your ways <u>for her</u> my ways," declares the Lord. "As the heavens are higher than the earth, so are my ways <u>for Emily</u> higher than your ways and my thoughts <u>about her education and life</u> than your thoughts." (Isaiah 55:8-9)

- Now tell God what your thoughts about the situation are. Try to be as specific and complete as possible. For example, you may think it's best for Emily to go to a school in your state because it is less expensive and she won't be as far from home. You think she should go to a Christian school. And you may think that a school in a certain size city or town would be best for her.

- Acknowledge to God that your thoughts and ways are not necessarily the same as His—that His are always higher than yours. Now ask Him what His thoughts about your situation are and what His ways in it are. Pause and be quiet for three to five minutes. Jot down ideas, Scriptures, impressions, song lyrics, memories, pictures, or any other thoughts that come to mind.

- Perhaps He has led you to new ways to pray about your situation—pray according to what He has shown you. If He has given you a Scripture to pray, use those words and biblical ideas in your prayer.

- Close your time by praising Him for who He is in regard to your need. Ask Him to reveal more of His will as days go by and to help you trust Him in it.

EXERCISE 2: Praying with Scripture and Relationship in Mind

Think about the situations you mentioned in Exercise 1.

1. Are there Scriptures that apply to the circumstances about which you are praying? Which ones? How do they affect your praying and confidence in praying?

2. Are you praying in relational dialogue with God, asking Him questions, gaining His perspective, telling Him about your doubts, fears, or disappointments as you wait on Him for His answers? Where would you like to grow in your dialogue with Him?

As you pray for these concerns this week, aim for a good balance of Scripture (reminding yourself and God of who He is and what He has said) and relationship (inviting Him to talk to you about what you are asking, what He is doing in that situation, and so on). Record any insights you have as you do this.

Afterward

I HAD NO IDEA WHEN I was writing this Bible study two years ago that God would use the ideas I was working with to take my ministry in a new direction. I'd been working in the area of prayer for ten years, passionate to help people connect with God relationally through two-way conversations with Him. People were eager to learn to communicate with Him this way. It was all good.

At the same time, however, I noticed a growing deficit in people's familiarity with Scripture. I had assumed that the people who came to my prayer retreats, read my prayer blogs, and used my Bible studies on prayer were reading God's Word regularly for themselves. I was often wrong. I had assumed that most of them were engaged in some kind of systematic Bible study. Again, I was frequently wrong. I had assumed that they were already hearing from God through Scripture in some fashion or other. I was often wrong about that, too. God helped me to see that if I was going to do effective prayer ministry, I also needed to help people learn to enjoy and depend on His Word.

Besides writing this Bible study, I wasn't sure what to do with that, since my calling at the time was as a prayer specialist at NavPress. My ministry focus was prayer, not Scripture. However, shortly after God began stirring these things in me, He very quickly and entirely to my surprise called me to a new place of service. I was offered a position as editorial director at Community Bible Study. I accepted and, as they say, the rest is history.

And so my two passions have come together. I get to help people engage with God through His Word—and I get to help them learn to talk to Him in two-way, relational conversation. I hope that this Bible study has helped you also to see the importance—and delight—of both.

Bible Reading Plan

IF WE WANT TO USE Scripture as a basis for conversation with God, then obviously we need some method of regularly spending time with Him and reading it. You may already have a plan for taking in His written Word each day. If you do, feel free to stick with that plan. But if you would like a suggestion for daily readings during the six weeks of this study, consider using the following plan. It is only a suggestion. Feel free to adapt it to whatever works best for you.

LESSON 1

Read Ephesians 1 every day this week. Choose from the following suggestions to assist you in your reading and praying.

- Is there a verse you'd like to turn into a prayer for yourself or someone else?
- Do you learn something about God that intrigues or delights you? Talk with Him about it.
- Notice the prayer Paul prays for the Ephesian believers at the end of the chapter. Ask God who needs that prayer. Then pray it for them, inserting their name(s) into it.
- Is there a blessing or truth in this chapter that you would like to receive? Talk to God about it. What would your life be like if you were really to receive and live by the truth He is offering?

What stands in your way of fully receiving it? Ask for His help and thank Him for His gift.

- Does anything in this passage trouble you? If so, tell God about it and ask Him for whatever you need in order to come to peace with what He says.

- Is there a verse you'd like to meditate on today? Write it onto a note card and carry it with you. Pull it out when you are waiting in line, stopped at a red light, or at other times when you have a spare moment.

LESSON 2

Read Ephesians 2 every day this week. Choose from the following suggestions to assist you in your reading and praying.

- What truth in this passage would you like to be reminded of more regularly? Ask the Holy Spirit to remind and prompt you about it until it becomes part of you.

- Is there something in this passage you don't fully understand? Tell God what confuses you. Then ask Him to interpret it to you through the Holy Spirit. Listen for what He says. He may reveal something right away. Or He may unfold it to you over the days and weeks to come—so keep listening.

- Remember that the Holy Spirit is your *paraclete* who comes alongside you in daily life. What self-reliance do you need to confess to God? And what portion of this chapter will you specifically ask Him to partner with you about today?

- Try praying this passage (or a shorter portion of it, such as verses 1-11 or 12-22) according to the method you used in the "Invite God to Speak" section of this lesson (also described in Appendix D).

• Is there a verse you'd like to memorize so that it is more readily available to the Holy Spirit to call to your mind when He wants to talk to you in the future?

LESSON 3

Read Ephesians 3 every day this week. Choose from the following suggestions to assist you in your reading and praying.

• Do you notice any verses that are especially encouraging when it comes to prayer? Thank God for the truth He is giving you and ask Him how He would like to make it more foundational in your conversations with Him. Write down what you sense Him saying and start practicing it with Him.

• Notice the prayer Paul prays at the end of the chapter. Ask God who you know who needs that prayer prayed for them. Then pray it for them, inserting their name(s) into it.

• Consider memorizing the prayer at the end of the chapter so you can pray it for yourself or others anytime, anywhere. Pray it for at least one person every day for the rest of this week.

• What do you notice about God's intentions and desires in this passage? Ask Him how He would like (a) for you to get on board with Him on these (then ask Him for help doing it) and (b) how you can pray for others with whom He also desires to partner in these ways.

• Thinking about how the enemy twists Scripture and tries to deceive us with it, what does God offer in this chapter that could serve as safeguards to such deception? Talk to Him about how He might want to establish these truths more firmly in your life.

LESSON 4

Read Ephesians 4 every day this week. Choose from the following suggestions to assist you in your reading and praying.

- As you read this chapter, invite the Holy Spirit to stir your emotions. What do you feel about what God is saying here? What emotions is He inviting you to share with Him? Talk to God about whatever He brings to light. Make sure to pray honestly from your heart—and then listen for Him to respond to you from His heart.

- How does this passage invite you to pray in bigger ways than you otherwise might? What prayer topics does this passage invite you to? If you were to pray these ways alongside of (or instead of) your usual way of praying, what would be different? Why not try it? Talk to God about what you notice.

- Does anything in this passage trouble you? If so, tell God about it and ask Him for whatever you need in order to come to peace with what He says. Make sure not to let the enemy twist anything or condemn or discourage you.

- Is there any "double-edged praying" you want to do based on this passage (see "Invite God to Speak" in Lesson 3). After you've prayed, invite God to talk to you about what you shared with Him.

- What do you notice about God's intentions and desires in this passage? Ask Him how He would like (a) for you to get on board with Him on these (then ask Him for help doing it) and (b) how you can pray for others with whom He also desires to partner in these ways.

- Is there a verse you'd like to meditate on today? Write it onto a note card and carry it with you. Pull it out when you are waiting in line, stopped at a red light, or at other times when you have a spare moment.

LESSON 5

Read Ephesians 5 every day this week. Choose from the following suggestions to assist you in your reading and praying.

- Before you read each day, pray the prayer from Psalm 119:18 that you used in the "Invite God to Speak" section of this week's lesson. After you finish reading, pause to reflect on the "wonderful things" God is saying to you through this passage. Thank Him for speaking to you.

- What does God say in this chapter that encourages you to pray differently and more broadly than you ordinarily might? Act on what He tells you and pray some of these more expansive prayers.

- Do you notice any verses that seem especially appropriate to turn into prayers? Thank God for the truth He is inviting you to and ask Him how He would like to make it part of your conversations and life with Him. Write down what you sense Him saying and start practicing it with Him.

- Is there something God says in this passage that is especially hard for you to believe or do? Talk to Him about why it is so hard. If you don't know, ask Him to show you what stands in the way. If you need to confess anything (such as fear, independence, or pride) do so. Receive His forgiveness. Then ask for whatever you need to move forward with Him on it. Don't forget to ask the Holy Spirit to come alongside you, providing whatever help you need.

- Try praying verses 15-21 according to the method you used in the "Invite God to Speak" section of this lesson (also described in Appendix D).

LESSON 6

Read Ephesians 6 every day this week. Choose from the following suggestions to assist you in your reading and praying.

- Think back to Lesson 3, where you learned how the enemy tries to twist Scripture in order to deceive, discourage, and defeat you. With these things in mind, meditate on verses 10-18. Ask God to show you what parts of the armor He especially wants you to focus on using today to protect you against the enemy's schemes. Then ask Him for the help you need according to what He showed you.

- Do you notice any verses in this chapter that apply directly to prayer? Ask the Holy Spirit how He would like you to use these verses today in your conversation with God.

- Is there something God says in this passage that is especially hard for you to believe or do? Talk to Him about why it is so hard. If you don't know, ask Him to show you what stands in the way. If you need to confess anything (fear, independence, pride, etc.), do so. Receive His forgiveness. Then ask for whatever you need to move forward with Him on it. Don't forget to ask the Holy Spirit to come alongside you, providing whatever help you need.

- What do you notice about God's intentions and desires in this passage? Ask Him how He would like (a) for you to get on board with Him on these (then ask Him for help doing it) and (b) how you can pray for others with whom He also desires to partner in these ways.

- Is there something in this passage you don't fully understand? Tell God what confuses you. Then ask Him to interpret it for you through the Holy Spirit. Listen for what He says. He may reveal something right away. Or He may unfold it to you over the days and weeks to come—so keep listening.

Suggestions for Meditating on God's Word

MEDITATING IS ANOTHER word for pondering. God promised blessing to Joshua if he would meditate on His Word (Joshua 1:8). And many times throughout the Psalms we are told of the joys and benefits of meditation—especially Psalm 119, which mentions at least eight times the good things that come from meditating on God's Word (verses 15, 23, 27, 48, 78, 97, 99, and 148). For many of us, meditating is a lost art. We move too fast; our lives are too full. There's too much noise, too much distraction, and too little ability to concentrate. But if we are to receive God's word in ways that bring life and transformation, we must learn to ponder and treasure it as David, Mary, and other biblical heroes did. Here are some suggestions I have found helpful.

Less is more. Although there is benefit to reading large passages of Scripture at a time, much can also be gained by reading just a verse or two in a sitting. The more I read, the more I'm likely to forget. But if I read just a verse or two, I am likely to read it a few times, think about it, perhaps pray about it, and remember it throughout the day. If your usual approach to Scripture is to read a chapter or two in the morning and then, more often than not, forget it by lunchtime, you might try reading just a couple of verses and intentionally try to keep them in mind throughout your day.

Mull it over. Let the ideas and truths of the verse(s) roll around in your head and heart. Ask the Holy Spirit to guide your ponderings. What would change if you were really to live the way His Word invites? How would you experience more life? How would those around you benefit? How would your relationship with God change? What might it cost to live this truth? What excites you? What causes you hesitation, reluctance, anxiety, or fear? Jot down your thoughts and feelings.

Ask questions. Questions will often arise as you meditate on God's Word. Notice in Luke 1 that both Zechariah and Mary had questions when they heard their respective messages. What are your questions? Go ahead and talk to God about them. Of course it's better if your questions come from a heart that wants to believe (like Mary's) than from one that already has decided what is possible and what is not (like Zechariah's), but either way it's better to ask your questions and keep the relationship and dialogue with God growing than to ignore them and shut down the conversation.

Memorize. When you commit God's Word to memory, you can ponder it anytime and anywhere: while standing in line, while waiting at traffic lights, or when you wake up in the middle of the night. Memorizing a passage also gives the Holy Spirit easy access to bring it to mind when circumstances and situations call for it. He'll be able to say to you, "Hey, remember? Here's a place you can put that truth into practice!"

Discuss it. Deuteronomy 6:5-9 seems to imply a connection between saturating oneself in the Word of God and loving Him heart, soul, and strength. One of the ways it suggests getting His Word into our hearts is by talking about it when sitting at home, walking along the way, when lying down and getting up. In other words, by making it a standard topic of everyday conversation. Do you have a friend or family member who is on the spiritual journey with you? Make it a point to talk with him or her about the Scriptures you are trying to receive.

Play "If . . ." As you ponder certain Scriptures, you may discover that even though you *want* to receive them, something seems to be preventing you. If that's the case, tell God your desire. Tell Him that you really want to receive His truth and be transformed by it. If you know what prevents you, tell Him that and ask Him to remove that hindrance.

Then play "If . . ." Ask Him to help you imagine what your life would be like *if* you were to receive His Word. For example, "If I were really to receive Your Word about You forgiving my sins and removing them from me as far as the east is from the west, then I would be so happy! I would feel like a ton of bricks had been lifted from me. Guilt and shame would be gone. I'd feel free again, like I'd been given a second chance. The heaviness would go. I'd sleep better at night. I'd be able to look certain people in the eye again. I'd be able to talk with You more openly. I wouldn't feel like I always had to hide and be afraid."

Tips on Listening to God

MANY OF THE "YOUR TURN" portions of each lesson ask you to listen for God's response, sense what He is saying, and interact with Him. If that type of prayer is new to you, don't let inexperience stop you from listening to God and beginning two-way conversations with Him. Here are some basics to guide you.

Expect God to speak to you. God speaks to all of His children, not just to certain "special" or extra-spiritual ones. "My sheep listen to my voice," Jesus said in John 10:27. And 1 Corinthians 2 says the Holy Spirit reveals to our spirits the very thoughts of God. So the starting place is to believe that God wants to talk with you and *will* talk to you.

Know what His voice is like. God speaks in many different ways, but the most common way is by His Holy Spirit speaking to your spirit through an inner, "still, small voice" (1 Kings 19:12, KJV). When I was just starting to actively listen for God, I expected His voice to be somehow louder or different or more distinct from the way my thoughts sounded. But I gradually learned that He most typically speaks to me by interjecting His thoughts into my own thoughts, sometimes with pictures, but most often in ways very similar to how my normal thinking goes. Expect God's "voice" to sound very similar to your own thoughts—except that what He has to say will be wiser, more creative, and all-around better.

Ask God to speak. Samuel, when he was first learning God's voice, gave Him an invitation: "Speak, for your servant is listening" (1 Samuel

3:10). Invite the Lord to speak to you too. Let Him know how much you desire two-way communication from Him.

Ask God to help you hear only Him. The enemy tries to get our ear. For that matter, our own thoughts and reasoning can sometimes compete with God's voice. But Jesus assures us that His sheep "will never follow a stranger; in fact, they will run away from him because they do not recognize a stranger's voice" (John 10:5). Ask God to protect your time of listening from distractions, including any voice that is not His.

Give Him time to speak. Sometimes, when I was starting out, I didn't hear God simply because I did not give Him time to speak. I'd ask a question or tell Him something and then move on to the next thing on my list, barely even pausing. When you speak to God, especially when you ask Him something, pause and wait quietly for His answer. Be still and notice what comes to you—thoughts, images, feelings, pictures, ideas, words or phrases, Scriptures, memories. These could very well be ways the Lord is responding to you.

Write down what you think He is saying. Recording what you hear is helpful for a variety of reasons. Writing helps you focus. It gives you a record of your conversation with God so you can better remember what He has said. It also provides a means of sharing what you are hearing with others so they can help discern if you are truly hearing from Him.

Don't worry! Trust God with the process. He wants to communicate with you even more than you want to hear from Him. As you seek to hear from Him with an open, submissive heart, you can count on Him to guide you and to protect you from getting off base.

What you are hearing should line up with God's written Word and with His character. If you doubt what you are hearing, ask God for confirmation, and perhaps share it with a friend who hears from God well. But don't assume that when you hear words of loving-kindness and affirmation that it's not God. He's your loving Father and truest Friend. If He says "I love you" or "I'm pleased with you" or "You're doing well" or "I want to bless you" or some other heartening words, don't discount them just because what He is saying encourages you! He's the God of all hope, comfort, and encouragement.

Get started. Like any other skill, listening to God takes practice. The best way to learn is by jumping in and doing it. He will help you. He will protect you. He will meet you where you are and move you forward into deeper communication with Him.

Lectio Divina

LECTIO DIVINA IS LATIN for "divine reading." It is a nearly 1,000-year-old Christian method of praying Scripture for the purpose of spiritual transformation. There are many different variations on the method, but most involve a four-step method of reading (or listening to) Scripture, with a different focus for each step. The four steps are these:

1. *Lectio*, which means "reading." In the early days, before everyone had the luxury of owning their own copy of the Scriptures, someone read or recited a short passage aloud while the others listened with full attention. For most of us today, this first step will involve a slow, careful, attentive reading of a short passage, perhaps six to ten verses at the most. Reading aloud is helpful to many people. To start, choose a narrative from the Gospels or a short section from the Psalms. After you have read or heard the passage, sit silently for three or four minutes. Allow the passage to unfold in your mind and heart.

2. *Meditatio* is the next step. It means "meditation." Read the passage again, and ponder what you are hearing. Does a word, phrase, image, or idea stick out to you? Stay with that thought; roll it over in your mind and heart. Don't try to figure out what it means, just focus on it and let it sink in.

3. *Oratio*, the third step, means "prayer." Read the passage again, and notice the feelings and emotions that rise in you. Allow

another three to four minutes of silence as the Holy Spirit stirs your heart. Then respond to God about what you are feeling. Tell Him about the desires, longings, fears, concerns, confusion, joy, sorrow (or whatever is stirred in you). Be honest and vulnerable. Take your time and sense His presence.

4. *Contemplatio* is the final step. It means "contemplation." In this step, you read the passage again and rest in it. The idea is to let whatever God has shown you to become part of you so that your heart is changed and you begin living from the truth He has revealed. Read the passage again. Sit silently for three or four minutes again. Then rest in His love, in His acceptance, in His direction for you. How will this revealed word play out in your life? Envision yourself living according to what He has shown you. Finish your time by inviting Him to take His Word deep into your life and to transform you accordingly.

Acknowledgments

I WANT TO EXPRESS my deep appreciation for the nine small group leaders and their small groups who piloted this Bible study so honestly and faithfully. They came from all over the country and represented different ages, ethnicities, denominations, and both genders. Each week they reported what had worked and what didn't. Their suggestions have made this Bible study a whole lot better.

I am also grateful to Connie Willems, my good friend and a most wonderful editor, who worked with me on this manuscript. We started working together more than ten years ago when we both served at NavPress. Now God has led each of us into new areas of ministry—but we have continued to share the same passion for connecting people with God relationally through prayer. It has been such a privilege to have her help to make this Bible study better.

The Author

CYNTHIA HYLE BEZEK is an author, editor, and prayer leader. She lives in Colorado Springs with her two cats and many friends. Widowed in 2008, Cynthia is mother to a wonderful grown son, Ian, with whom she enjoys taking active vacations, usually to Spanish-speaking countries.

Cynthia currently serves as editorial director for Community Bible Study in Colorado Springs. Prior to that, she worked at NavPress, overseeing their prayer resources and before that, editing *Pray!* magazine.

She is the author of *Prayer Begins with Relationship, Knowing the God You Pray To,* and *Come Away with Me:* Pray! *Magazine's Guide to Prayer Retreats.*

Cynthia is available to lead prayer retreats that help participants to learn to dialogue with God in two-way conversation, and relate to Him more closely. You can learn more about her and read her blog at http://cynthiaprayblog.wordpress.com.

PRAYER STUDIES

from
Cynthia Hyle Bezek

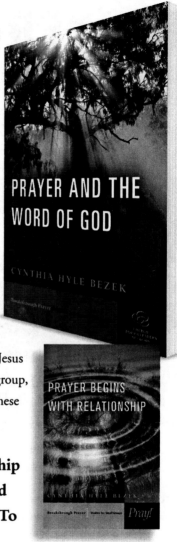

PRAYER AND THE WORD OF GOD

Prayer and the Word of God is a part of a three-book Breakthrough Prayer series by Cynthia. Each six-week study will teach the user something significant about his or her prayer relationship with Jesus Christ. Challenge and equip your small group, Sunday school class or Bible study with these solid, basic truths about prayer.

PRAYER BEGINS WITH RELATIONSHIP

Prayer Begins with Relationship
Prayer and the Word of God
Knowing the God You Pray To
(Available late 2014)

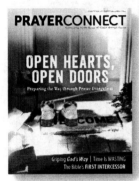

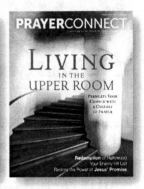

CPSIA information can be obtained
at www.ICGtesting.com
Printed in the USA
FFOW05n1520260614

9 781935 012542